Old TAYPORT

by
Mairi Shiels

The Cynicus Publishing Company operated in Tayport from 1902 until 1911. Martin Anderson, the owner of the company, was already well known in London literary circles for his social and political cartoons. When he returned to Tayport, he designed greetings cards, invitations and advertisements, but it was his colourful postcards which were to bring him fame and fortune. Superbly drawn, his cynical (hence the name Cynicus) and extremely funny designs enjoyed enormous popularity in the pre-First World War years when up to a million postcards a day were being sent. One of the company's very successful sales ploys was to produce cards showing anonymous locations to which any place name could be added. This one is a fine example – vaguely resembling the view of Castle Street from Broad Street where the company premises were, 'Our Village' could represent many other places in Britain equally well.

First published in the United Kingdom, 1998,
by Stenlake Publishing
Telephone / Fax: 01290 551122

ISBN 1 84033 050 3

ACKNOWLEDGEMENTS

The author would like to thank Jim Kinnear for his advice.

The publishers would like to thank Ian Lindsay for allowing the use of his
collection of postcards and photographs of Tayport in this book.

The publishers regret that they cannot supply
copies of any pictures featured in this book.

Everybody's
Doing it
at TAYPORT

No one escaped Martin Anderson's entertaining social comment. Lovers, politicians, holiday-makers and children all provided inspiration for Cynicus. His cards brought colour and humour into lives which were very often grim and grey, and the business expanded steadily to become one of the principal employers in Tayport. Success, however, was to be short-lived, and as the craze for sending and collecting postcards began to diminish, so too did the fortunes of the Cynicus Publishing Company. By 1911 financial problems had forced it to close down. Cynicus did try to set up in business elsewhere, but to no avail. Castle Cynicus, his beloved mansion which he had built on the hill above Balmullo, gradually fell into disrepair and was demolished in 1939.

INTRODUCTION

Much evidence has been gathered to indicate that the area around Tayport has been settled since earliest times. Tentsmuir has yielded stone arrowheads and clay pottery dating from the Stone Age, and evidence of smelting furnaces from the Bronze Age. Discovery of many of their coins near Leuchars would indicate the presence of Romans in the vicinity, and during the ninth and tenth centuries the area was subjected to numerous Viking raids.

From the Middle Ages onwards there is documentation referring to the ferry crossing at Tayport. In those early days there was no pier or slipway from which to load boats. Instead embarking and disembarking were done from a rock or craig, hence the settlement's early name of Ferryport-on-Craig. This was the most easterly crossing point on the river, and being shorter than those immediately up river at Newport, Woodhaven and Balmerino, the ferry was well used. Around 1455 James II recognised its strategic importance by building castles both at Tayport and Broughty Ferry. The last remains of the castle were removed in the 1850s and a house built on the site.

A thriving little community gradually developed around the ferry and the castle, mainly in the area of Tay Street and Dalgliesh Street. Despite extensive rebuilding in this area, it is still possible to gain an impression of what a close-knit community it must have been. By the start of the nineteenth century, the village was spreading south into the area of Nelson Street and Ogilvy Street. Many of the inhabitants made a living from the sea, either as boatmen or as fishermen engaged in gathering mussels, whelks or salmon. There was considerable employment in agriculture, but possibly the most lucrative employment in the eighteenth century was weaving and spinning for Dundee merchants.

The parish of Ferryport-on-Craig was established in 1606, and the church erected in 1607. The parish consisted of the lands of Scotscraig Estate and the village. Scotscraig Estate dates back to the early twelfth century and close links were always maintained between village and estate.

In the early 1800s the ferry was facing much competition, both from the bridge at Perth and from the more efficient ferries at Newport and Woodhaven. Although it was still used by drovers, happy to take advantage of the good pasturage on both sides of the crossing, by 1830 even this trade had died out as a result of the new steamboat being used on the Newport crossing.

It was the arrival of the railway in 1848 which led to the development of the modern village of Tayport. The railway and the new harbour built by the railway company brought increased employment opportunities as industry developed. The village was renamed Tayport, as the earlier name was considered too cumbersome for station boards and railway timetables. Although some through trade was inevitably lost after the building of the railway bridge in 1878, both the harbour and the village continued to flourish. Between the 1860s and the early 1900s a wide variety of industries was established – spinning, weaving, engineering, timber handling, bobbin making, printing and the manufacture of aerated water.

In 1887 Tayport acquired the status of a police burgh, and thereafter the affairs of the burgh were managed by the town council. Two early achievements of the council were the installation of a pure water supply with a sewage and drainage system, and the making up and paving of the roads and pathways in the burgh. Throughout the twentieth century much of the council's energies were concentrated on improving housing, as substandard buildings were removed and large numbers of council houses erected. All these efforts without doubt improved the general level of health and appearance of the village.

In the last twenty or thirty years Tayport has seen further change. The opening of the Tay Road Bridge in 1966 certainly affected the village, and with Dundee so much closer, many local businesses suffered. The railway is no more, and the harbour is now almost entirely given over to pleasure craft. Huge new housing developments have appeared, many of them private. Although many of the old industries are gone, those which remain continue to do well, and the village is continuing to develop its holiday and leisure facilities. Despite all the change Tayport has managed to retain its own identity, and can look to the future confident of its ability to adapt to changing circumstances.

BATTENBURG TERRACE, TAYPORT

This Edwardian postcard shows the section of Albert Street which, until the First World War, was known as Battenburg Terrace. In the rush of anti-German feeling that accompanied the outbreak of war, the German-sounding name was dropped. In the royal family, the name Battenburg was changed to the English form Mountbatten.

In 1887 Tayport was established as a police burgh, and from then until local government reorganisation in 1975 the elected town council managed the affairs of the burgh. To begin with, council meetings were held in chambers in Castle Street, in part of the building now occupied by Morning, Noon and Night. Space was limited there and in 1899 these buildings on the corner of William Street and Reform Street were acquired. They served as the burgh chambers until 1953, when the chambers were moved to Kilmaron House on Queen Street. During World War Two one of the council's functions was to organise and co-ordinate the various defence measures necessary in the burgh. For the duration of the war therefore, part of the William Street chambers became the Air Raid Precautions centre and also the headquarters for the company of the Home Guard which operated in the district.

The Braes was the name popularly given to the West Common, the narrow, rugged strip of land that stretches along the shore west of the old harbour towards the lighthouses. Wellcraig, the house in the picture, is considered locally – but questionably – to be the most northerly in Fife. The lemonade factory, usually remembered as Melville's, is on the right. Christopher Melville was a Castle Street grocer who started his aerated water business in Dalgleish Street in 1900. The business was in operation until 1957, although for the last twenty years it was owned by Kidd and Co. Even as late as the 1950s, the factory was still using water from a local well for their production.

THE BRAES AND PUTTING GREEN, TAYPORT.

99747 (JV)

The small hut in the foreground of this 1931 picture belonged to the swimming club and was erected for the convenience of the lady bathers. The West Common was popular with bathers in the summer and bramble-pickers in the autumn, although blackberrying was perhaps a safer pastime; according to the town council minutes, danger signs with lifebuoys were erected at both the East and West Lights as early as 1899. After World War Two the swimming club gave the shed to the Tayport Violet Football Club, to be re-erected on the East Common as a changing room. The putting green, in the background, was a popular feature of the West Common both before and after the Second World War. In just ten days during the summer of 1923 it was used by 2,930 people! Players had spectacular views, but in such an exposed situation a round must have been bracing at the best of times. The post-war development of the East Common, with its more varied recreational facilities, led to a decline in use of the green.

THE WEST LIGHTS, TAYPORT   033

In previous years the lighting and buoying of the river were the responsibility of the Fraternity of Masters and Seamen in Dundee. Their headquarters were in Trinity House, a fine building demolished in the 1880s to make way for the West Station, itself later demolished to allow construction of the road bridge access roads. In 1823 Trinity House, as the Fraternity was commonly known, established both the East and the West Lights on the south shore of the estuary. Later in the nineteenth century the Fraternity's responsibilities were gradually transferred to the Dundee Harbour Board. The area around the West Light was known as Tayside, and the group of cottages in this picture all date from the first half of the nineteenth century.

East Light, Tayport

The East Light's period of operation was short-lived. With the building of the new harbour in the 1840s, river traffic into Tayport increased considerably, but as a result of shifting sand and silt, the navigation channel altered. The practice of lining up the shorter East Light with the taller West Light was no longer a practical navigation guide, and so the Pile Light was constructed out in the river, thus making the East Light redundant.

Harbour, Tayport

The fine harbours at Tayport and Broughty Ferry were constructed by the Edinburgh, Perth and Dundee Railway Company after they had built the railway to Tayport in 1848. The opening of the new harbour vastly increased the volume of Tayport's shipping business, and steamships of a considerable size were able to discharge and load their cargoes there. Contrary to the impression given by this fairly deserted picture, Tayport enjoyed a trading heyday in the latter years of the nineteenth and the early years of this century, and the harbour was frequently filled with both steam and sailing ships, sometimes two or three abreast.

10

THE HARBOUR, TAYPORT

The vessel on the right is a puffer, one of the tiny steamships used for mussel dredging, or 'the Draig' as it was known locally. Dredging had been carried out here for centuries, and there were often as many as sixty or seventy men involved in the industry, both on the mussel scalps (beds) out on the river and on the foreshore. Mussel dredging was extremely hard, dirty work, but the introduction of steam for propelling the little boats and working the dredging apparatus improved matters considerably. In the pre-trawling days of line fishing, mussels were used as bait for white fish. Fishing smacks from further south, *en route* for northern waters, would call at Tayport to collect their bait. Mussel dredging here had almost completely ceased by the outbreak of World War Two.

This aerial view shows one of Tayport's major imports being unloaded. Much of the timber arriving at the harbour came from Baltic ports, and although some was taken by rail to other destinations, the bulk of it was destined for Donaldson's sawmill, just out of sight to the left of the harbour. James Donaldson started trading in the town in 1860 and expanded considerably over the years, until by the 1920s the company was the largest timber merchant in Fife. Sometimes the timber cargoes were unloaded directly into the water, then floated in raft formation round to the beach beside the sawmill. The mill closed in 1983, and for many years before that had been the only regular commercial user of the harbour.

The proximity of the station to the harbour, illustrated in this 1908 picture, encouraged the import of goods destined for further afield in Fife. In particular, from the end of the nineteenth century onwards, there were considerable imports of raw materials for the Fife paper mills – esparto grass from Spain and North Africa, wood pulp from the Baltic and china clay from the south of England – although after World War Two this trade tended to use the harbour at Methil. During the Second World War, the railway link to Leuchars was particularly important to the RAF as the harbour was used as headquarters of their Air-Sea Rescue Unit. Servicemen repaired and improved the inner slipway at the harbour so that it was suitable for their powerful motor boats, and the area was the scene of much activity. The RAF buildings remained at the harbour for many years after the war, and were even considered for conversion to housing during the shortage of the immediate post-war years.

Harbour, Tayport

The vessel pictured here is the *Dolphin*, which served as the ferry-boat to Broughty Ferry for many years before being taken out of service in 1920. Ferries had crossed the river here for hundreds of years, but with the introduction of steamships in the 1820s, Newport emerged as the most important crossing point. Although a steamship, the *Mercury*, was also introduced on the Tayport crossing in 1839, it provided a fairly irregular service and posed little threat to the Newport ferry. The coming of the railway in 1848 and the building of the new harbour restored Tayport's importance. The railway company established the world's second railway ferry, or 'floating railway', by which whole trains were transported across the river on specially designed ferry-boats.

Tayport's pre-eminence as a ferry crossing was short-lived, however, as the opening of the Tay Railway Bridge in 1878 inevitably resulted in passengers bypassing the town. Even the Tay Bridge disaster of 1879, when the train ferry was temporarily reinstated, only provided a brief respite for Tayport. Nevertheless, despite the fall in demand, the railway company, who had acquired the ferry rights in the 1840s, were still obliged to provide a service. Despite several attempts on their behalf to discontinue the ferry-boat, strong local opposition ensured its continuation. The *Dolphin* and the *Royal Norman* were the last two regular ferry-boats.

An accident at the harbour coal-drop. From its earliest days, one of Tayport harbour's main functions was to allow the loading of coal, both for export and to power the steamships working off the east coast. The railway provided a link with the Fife coalfields, and a coal-drop was constructed at the east end of the harbour to facilitate loading. Coal loaded in Tayport was cheaper than in Dundee, probably by about ten shillings a wagon, so ships naturally preferred to use Tayport. At busy spells loading continued both day and night, and in 1904 the town council received noise complaints about the trawlers whistling during the night.

The original coal-drop was made of wood, but this was considered unsafe and in 1910 was replaced with a much more substantial iron structure mounted on a massive stone base. Despite rigorous weight tests at the time of its construction, there were, according to local newspapers, 'at least two occasions when runaway wagons landed on the decks of trawlers'. These two pictures show such an occasion, but no date for the accident can be ascertained.

In 1848 the Edinburgh, Perth and Dundee Railway Company extended their line from Leuchars into Tayport. After the Tay Railway Bridge was opened in 1878, the town was linked to Dundee by the new bridge and the connecting line through Newport. At the height of the railway's popularity, there were frequent services over the bridge to Dundee, and to Edinburgh and the south, both by the main line and also by the coastal route via St Andrews and Crail. Gradually, increasing dependence on road transport spelled the end for Tayport's railway connections. The link to Leuchars was closed in the winter of 1957-58, and the building of the Tay Road Bridge and its approach roads in 1966 necessitated the closure of the line from Newport to Tayport. For three months after the closure of the line, and before the opening of the bridge, rail passengers were taken between Tayport and Newport by bus.

This late Victorian view, looking west, shows the station before the south platform was covered over. Following the closure of Tayport Station in 1966, the ground was cleared and council houses built on the site. Their name, President Grant Place, commemorates the visit of the President of the United States to Tayport in 1877 to view the new bridge. He arrived from Edinburgh by train and was taken out to the bridge by the tug *Excelsior*. Another less publicised event occurred in 1881 just two hundred yards south of the station. A slow train from Burntisland ran into a goods train, telescoping two carriages and killing six people. One suggested cause of the crash was human error, resulting from the sixteen-hour shifts being worked by the elderly signalman. After the accident, shifts were shortened. Just two years later the station burned down, but was speedily rebuilt. The same fate befell Leuchars station, although it was fired intentionally by Suffragettes as part of their pre-First World War campaign for the vote.

Castle Street and Castle Terrace, Tayport.

75089. (J.V.)

The name Castle Street is a reminder of the castle, which was built about 1455. It stood on the high ground above the old harbour and would have commanded a fine view of the entrance to the river. The last remains were demolished in the 1850s and the appropriately named Castle Cottage now occupies the site. Two long-established Tayport businesses can be seen on the right of this picture. The branch of William Low occupied these premises from 1894 until 1969. James Redpath provided gardening services and sold produce from his home, latterly in Ogilvy Street, from the 1880s. He opened his Castle Street shop in 1908, and in 1911 his son John established the Burnbank Nurseries in the Scotscraig Smithy on the Cupar Road. They are still owned by the family today.

CASTLE ST. TAYPORT.

The date 1908 and the letters PB worked into the stone on the building in the foreground reveal exactly when these premises were built for Peebles Brothers, the Dundee grocers. Many of their other branches were built in the same style, using red sandstone, which contrasts markedly with the whinstone of the earlier buildings beyond. Peebles Brothers operated from this shop until 1959. Next door was Edward Wilkie the draper, here until the 1960s, and Wedderspoon the butcher, another well-known Tayport business. The Buttercup Dairy van must have been visiting the village, as there was never a branch of this famous company in Tayport.

Post Office, Tayport

This building housed the post office from the 1890s until 1939. After that various shops occupied the premises until fairly recently, when it was converted into a house. The small shop next door is now a charity shop, but in this 1930s view it was occupied by James Brown tailor, also apparently the agent for Pullars of Perth.

This baker's delivery van belonged to Robert Ferguson of 27 Castle Street. Prior to opening in Castle Street in 1894, he had a shop in Whitenhill. In 1924 he was joined in the business by Daniel Dunnett, and Ferguson and Dunnett traded until the 1930s. The sharp-eyed will recognise these houses as being on Craig Road. Ferguson and Dunnett also had a shop at the top of Newport High Street.

The 1872 Education Act legislated for school boards to be established to oversee education in every parish, and as a result of the Tayport School Board's efforts, this school was opened in 1876. Prior to 1872 there had been at least four schools in the village. One of these was the old subscription school, further up William Street, which is still in use today as the nursery school. This photograph is quite different from the posed school groups with which we are more familiar; the children look very relaxed, with many of the boys trying to gain the best vantage point for the camera.

Unlike the front, the back view of Tayport School has changed completely. From very early on it became clear that space was at a premium, and as the twentieth century progressed accommodation became a real problem. In 1926 Sir James Scott wrote that 'a more open and commodious site should have been chosen where buildings could have been erected and added'. The problem was solved by various extensions and alterations, in particular the large 1936 extension which covers the entire back face of the building. At a time when the school was still providing a full education until third year in secondary, the extra space must have been particularly welcome for the specialist and practical secondary subjects. As a further solution to the problem, the infant classes were housed in the old subscription school for most of this century.

Established Church, Tayport

The old parish church was built in 1607. By the late eighteenth century its condition was deteriorating rapidly, and Dr Robert Dalgleish, Laird of Scotscraig and also parish minister, had the building restored, with further improvements being made in 1825. The proprietors of Scotscraig were closely linked with the church – in the eighteenth century they paid most of the minister's stipend, sat in the enclosed pew in front of the gallery, with room behind for their servants, and between lengthy morning and afternoon services they would have lunch in a small room in the tower. In 1979 it was decided to unite the church with Queen Street church, and although the old church is no longer used for regular services it is well worth a visit. The graveyard is full of interesting old stones, an unmarked one for Cynicus, reflecting the poverty of his later years, and others telling of the many Tayport men lost at sea.

Free Church, Tayport.

In 1843 the Church of Scotland experienced the Disruption, when ministers all over Scotland left their churches to establish the Free Church of Scotland, taking many members of their congregations with them. The Rev. Nicolson of Tayport was one of these ministers. The new Free Church congregation in Tayport was so enthusiastic that its members quarried and dressed the stones for the new church at a quarry on Scotscraig Estate themselves, and then built the church on Queen Street with the help of their womenfolk. The present façade, bell tower, transept, hall and organ are all later additions. The Church of Scotland and the Free Church reunited in 1929, and this church has been the parish church since 1979.

ERSKINE UNITED FREE CHURCH TAYPORT

Rev. Alexander Horne

This church in Castle Street, also dating from 1843, was originally the United Presbyterian Church. In 1900 the UP joined with the Free Church to become the United Free Church. Tayport then had two free churches, the Erskine (above) and the Queen Street. In 1929 the Free Church and the Church of Scotland reunited, so there were then three Church of Scotland buildings! At that time a group who wished to adhere to the old Free Church principles, broke away and established a new Free Church in King Street in 1931. The Erskine Church was in use until the 1960s when it was sold, first of all to be used as a printing works, and latterly as a heating showroom.

The Tayport Episcopal Church Sunday School enjoying their annual picnic, probably around 1910. Unfortunately the location is unknown. Sunday best was the order of the day for such occasions, but there must have been many a muddy knee and torn petticoat on the way home. The Episcopal Church in Queen Street was built in 1898; the Catholic Church, dating from 1938, stands further along the street. Perhaps Church Street would have been a more appropriate name for Queen Street.

THE COMMON, TAYPORT

A view of the East Common from around the turn of the century, before the area was developed. In 1799 an agreement was reached with Robert Dalgliesh of Scotscraig giving the villagers of Tayport access to three pieces of common ground – the East and West Commons and the Cross Greens. Traditionally villagers enjoyed certain privileges on these lands, such as the right to graze their cattle, to steep and dry lint, to wash and bleach clothes and flax, and to cut divots for thatching their houses. By the start of the twentieth century the villagers were rarely exercising any of their traditional rights, and instead were using the commons more and more for leisure purposes. Beyond the railway can be seen evidence of Tayport's industrial development. Spinning, weaving and engineering works were all established here in the latter half of the nineteenth and the early twentieth centuries.

Over a remarkably short period of time the East Common was transformed from an area of marsh, whins and rough ground to a well cared for recreation ground. An extensive programme of rubbish dumping levelled out the land, and although this policy caused much controversy, it did allow the area to be properly landscaped. The play area, boating pond and adjacent putting green all proved extremely popular, and the boating pond doubled as a skating rink in winter. The putting green was extended from nine to eighteen holes just after World War Two. This extension caused an increase in prices, but in the immediate post-war years entertainment was still cheap – a round costing 2d could be followed by half an hour on the boating pond for 3d. There has always been a football pitch laid out on the common, and Tayport footballers have enjoyed tremendous success over the years. For much of this century there was a cricket pitch, and for some time a hockey pitch too.

CRAIG ROAD AND WAR MEMORIAL, TAYPORT.

85936

The war memorial was planned immediately after World War One, and as well as the impressive entrance was to include a memorial garden and bowling green. By 1923 the gardens had been laid out and opened, and the following year the bowling green and pavilion were completed. In 1950 the memorial was visited by the Queen (now Queen Mother) during her tour of North Fife burghs. Craig Road, on the left, was previously known as Scotscraig Road.

BOWLING GREEN, TAYPORT.

This early picture shows the memorial garden and bowling green before the hedge between the two had grown to form a screen. Once completed the town council took over responsibility for the upkeep of the garden, bowling green and the houses which also formed part of the memorial. There had previously been other attempts to form a bowling club, and in the early years of this century when the tennis courts were experiencing a less popular spell, work was even started on converting them to a bowling green. Fortunately for the tennis club, that plan came to nothing.

CUPAR ROAD, TAYPORT.

Tayport's streets were formerly illuminated by gas lamps, such as the one visible in this picture. The town's gasworks were at the bottom of Mill Lane beside the railway, and were bought over by the town council in 1909. Gas lighting involved considerable work, with the lighting of individual lamps each night, and the summertime removal and cleaning of the glass lanterns. Electricity came to Tayport in 1929 but it was not until after World War Two that the first electric street lights were installed. Even then, post-war fuel restrictions limited their use considerably. They were so effective however, that complaints were received by the town council from Dundee Harbour Authority that the new lights were hindering navigation on the Tay! After a boat trip by town councillors the offending lights were shaded.

QUEEN STREET, TAYPORT.

THIS IS A REAL PHOTO

This pre-war photograph was taken by Dundee photographer R.H. Lundie. Out of sight in the gap between the houses on the left is the Episcopal Church, built in 1898. Slightly further along the street is the building which was once the Picture House. This started life as the Drill or Volunteer Hall, but it is recorded in the town council minutes that by the end of the First World War it was being used for 'cinematograph performances'. Briefly called the Empire Hall in the 1920s, it soon became the Picture House. Despite a serious fire in 1946, it was immediately reconstructed and continued as a place of entertainment until the 1960s.

Nelson Street, Tayport

40831

Valentines Series

Looking up Nelson Street in the early years of the century. The shop across the end of the street was later demolished to allow easier access to Maitland Street. Scott and Fyfe's first weaving factory, established in the 1860s, stood at the bottom of Nelson Street on the left; James Scott's engineering works, established in 1870, were on the right. James Scott, later Sir James, was Tayport's provost from 1890 until 1896, the second person to hold the post. Scott and Fyfe were originally linen weavers but, as markets changed, they progressed to jute weaving. They continued to move with the times and their innovative approach, combined with their willingness to diversify into production of many modern textiles, has ensured their continued success to the present day.

MARSHALL PLACE
NELSON STREET
TAYPORT

It is now extremely difficult to recognise the stretch of Nelson Street that includes Marshall Place. The central building was named Marshall Place after its owner of 100 years ago, John Marshall. The building on the right started life as the Mission Hall but from the early 1900s housed the Guardbridge Co-operative shop. Now both buildings are well disguised behind the modern Co-op shop frontage.

40330

Elizabeth Street was the last of these three fine wide streets to be developed. Like Nelson Street and Ogilvy Street it originally extended only from Cross Street to Pond Lane. In order to extend it towards Queen Street in the early years of the century, it was necessary to bridge the Scotscraig Burn and also knock down the dwelling house which stood in the way, seen here at the top of the street. Also visible in this picture is the developing Craig Road on the hillside – at the turn of the century Tayport was rapidly spreading upwards as well as outwards.

Elizabeth Street, Tayport

Although perhaps not obvious in the previous picture, the well-finished and tidy appearance of the streets in many of these photographs bears witness to the huge efforts of the town council in the early years of this century to make up and pave the paths and streets. Even after they had been tarred maintenance was a continual job, with frequent use of the water cart required in the summer months to keep the dust down – an operation enjoyed by the local children. Weeding of the streets had to be done fairly regularly, usually by women, in the days before there was sufficient traffic to do the job automatically.

TENNIS COURTS, TAYPORT.

The tennis club was first formed in the 1880s and has certainly had its ups and downs. In the early 1900s the club was wound up altogether, with the town council taking over the grounds in 1902 and planning alternative use of the land as a bowling green. Although the green did not materialise, the tennis club experienced more difficulties between the wars, and it was not until after World War Two that the sport gained more interest and popularity. The council then carried out much needed improvements, relaying the surface and replacing nets and fencing. This 1950s picture illustrates the tremendous changes in style and fashion even since then.

CURLING AT TAYPORT, NEAR DUNDEE.

Copyright

The Scotscraig Curling Club was another long established club in the village, with many enjoying the 'roaring game'. In the 1920s there was also a separate ladies club. This picture shows a busy day at the pond behind the tennis courts. It was in use from the 1880s, but before that the curlers used the Garpit pool, now a hollow on the golf course. Although the curling club continued, outdoor curling at Tayport more or less ceased after World War Two. The curling pond, tennis courts and present-day play-park are all laid out on the Cross Greens, another of the village's common areas.

Scotscraig Golf Club House, Tayport.

75090. J.V.

Golf has long been a popular Tayport pastime with both young and old, as this 1913 picture shows. Scotscraig Golfing Club has the distinction of being one of the oldest in the world (either the twelfth or fourteenth; it is unclear which). The original club was formed in 1817 and members played on a very limited six-hole course at the Garpit. These early players observed very stringent dress rules. The uniforms for playing and for ceremonial use were equally colourful and splendid, and any violation of the dress rules incurred a fine of two bottles of port. This old club flourished for over twenty years until the Garpit farmer ploughed up the land! A renewed interest in the game in the 1880s led to the re-forming of the club under the leadership of Admiral Dougall, Laird of Scotscraig. After much negotiation and hard work a new nine-hole course was opened in 1888. In 1890 the Scotscraig members were joined by members from the Newport club, their course by then being defunct. This large increase in membership created a need for improved premises, and in 1896 the fine clubhouse shown here was opened.

Scotscraig Golf Club, Tayport

The club has continued to expand throughout this century. In 1904 further ground was leased from Scotscraig permitting the extension of the course to eighteen holes, and in 1907 the clubhouse was extended to provide accommodation for the ladies, who had been accepted for membership since 1896. In 1923 the club was able to purchase all the land on which the course was laid out. The steadily rising membership and the growing popularity of the game necessitated further extensions of the clubhouse, the major one of the 1930s shown in this photograph, plus more recent additions to cater for the 700-plus members which the club now has. In the background on the left of this picture is the Abertay Foundry. This business, run for many years by the Scott Brothers, sons of James Scott, was trading as the Hillside Foundry when it finally closed.

The Scotscraig Smiddy on the Cupar Road is still easily recognisable today. It was run by at least four generations of the Johnstone family, and this picture shows James Young Johnstone (born 1879) shoeing a horse, with his father William Johnstone (born 1846) standing second from the right with his hands on his hips. The blacksmith and his family lived in the cottage that adjoined the smiddy. By 1911 the Johnstones had moved their home and business into Tayport where it was located near the station, and the cottage and former smiddy were occupied by John Redpath, who established the Burnbank Nursery on the premises. The nursery is still owned and worked by his family. On William Johnstone's death, Edward (Ted) Johnstone, aged fourteen, began to work with his father James as a blacksmith. The business survived until just after the Second World War when increasing farm mechanisation led to a decline in the use of horses. At one stage the smiddy had forged golf club heads which were sent to St Andrews for finishing and shafting.

CRAIGWHINNIE, TAYPORT.

When James Wallace retired in 1895 he had of course to give up his occupancy of the smithy cottage. He was clearly well thought of, as Craigwhinnie, just across the road, was built for him. Scotscraig Estate gifted the land, the quarry at Kirktonbarns donated the stone, and perhaps other materials were contributed as gifts too. 'J.W. 1895' is worked into the stonework below the eaves, and Mr Wallace lived there until his death in 1915. Apart from his trade as blacksmith, James Wallace was also the local bone-setter, and this may have partly accounted for his importance in the community. Although by the late nineteenth century there were growing numbers of properly qualified doctors and nurses, there were still a number of other people to whom ordinary people would apply for help with medical problems. The services for example of the midwife, the worm-doctor or the bone-setter were frequently called upon. In times when so much work was of a manual nature involving hard physical labour, many of the resulting aches, pains and injuries could be eased by a skilled bone-setter. The bone-setter usually had another occupation, very often blacksmith, so James Wallace was typical in this respect.

Scotscraig House, Tayport

Scotscraig Estate dates back to the twelfth century. It was owned in the thirteenth century by Sir Michael Scott (hence Scott's Craig) and in the seventeenth century by Archbishop Sharp, who was murdered on Magus Muir during the time of the Covenanters. Between 1740 and 1840 the estate was owned by Rev. William and Rev. Robert Dalgliesh, father and son. It was Robert who in 1806 had this new mansion built to replace an older building close by. The next owners were the Maitland Dougalls, who for over fifty years maintained close links with the village. In 1918 the estate was bought by the Corporation of Dundee. The Dundee Directory of that year explained that the land would be 'industrially developed, and the timber, with which the land is thickly covered, used for building purposes'. Fortunately these plans were not implemented, and much of the estate was sold back to a private owner in 1925. After World War Two the house fell into disrepair, and has now been demolished.

Fife Fox-Hounds at Scotscraig.

This picture of the local hunt at Scotscraig is unfortunately not dated, but the dress of the young lads in the foreground would suggest the Edwardian era. Under the proprietorship of the Maitland Dougalls the villagers enjoyed free access to the grounds of Scotscraig Estate, and on Mrs Maitland Dougall's death in 1900 the town council minuted their appreciation of this privilege.

39975 JV   "JESS PHILP'S DAM, TAYPORT."

Jess Philp's dam, on the back road to Newport. At the end of the nineteenth century, when there was much controversy about how best to acquire a fresh water supply for the village, one solution considered was to use the area around this dam as the catchment area for Tayport's water supply. In 1888, however, the newly formed town council decided that the cheapest and most efficient solution was to do as Newport had done, and bring water over the railway bridge from Dundee. This was followed by the implementation of an effective drainage and sewerage scheme. Both these measures immediately improved the general health of the villagers.

Old FERRYDEN

by
Fiona Scharlau

Montrose photographer Ken Hay took this photograph before the oil base was constructed. The eighteenth century pier (foreground) has now been extended to accommodate large vessels such as the *Big Orange XVIII* (painted blue in January 2002!) and other oil support vessels.

Not all men in Ferryden went to sea. Many stayed on dry land to provide support services for the fishing fleet, including this net mender.

© Angus Council Cultural Services 2002
First published in the United Kingdom, 2002,
by Stenlake Publishing
Telephone / Fax: 01290 551122

ISBN 1 84033 197 6

With the exception of the pictures on pages 2, 11, 32, 37, 40 and 46, which have been reproduced by courtesy of Tom Valentine, all the images in this book are from the collection of Angus Council Cultural Services. If you would like copies of any of these pictures, please contact: Angus Local Studies Centre, Montrose Library, 214 High Street, Montrose, DD10 9RS. www.angus.gov.uk/history

ACKNOWLEDGEMENTS

The author would like to thank the staff of Cultural Services and the Angus Local Studies Centre for their help and moral support. Thanks are also gratefully extended to John and Wilma Thomson, Norman Atkinson, Margaret King, Daniel West, Tom Valentine, Malcolm Archibald of the East of Scotland Fisheries Project, Keith Parsonson, Ken Hay and numerous other Ferrydeners.

FURTHER READING

The books listed below were used by the author during her research. None of them are available from Stenlake Publishing. Those interested in finding out more are advised to contact their local bookshop or reference library.

Statistical Account of Scotland
New Statistical Account of Scotland
Andrew Douglas, A History of Ferryden, 1855
D. H. Edwards, Amongst the Fisherfolk of Ferryden & Usan, 1921
Joe West & Dorothy Morrison, Old Ferryden, 1985
Joe West, A Personal History of Ferryden, n.d.
Dorothy Morrison, Montrose Lifeboat 200 Years of Service, 2000
Jackson & Lyhte ed., The Port of Montrose, 1993
Agnes Butterfield, Hercules Ross (unpublished)
Angus County Council records
Montrose Review
Angus Local Studies Centre files

INTRODUCTION

Ferryden is a picturesque village situated on the south side of the River South Esk, near where the river meets the North Sea. It looks across to its larger neighbour Montrose, separated by the river but linked by a bridge.

Ferryden was once a major fishing port but owes its existence to an ancient river crossing. The road from the south emerged in the vicinity of the pier and a ferry provided the means of crossing over to the royal burgh of Montrose and journeying onwards to the north. The earliest mention of the ferry is in 1178 when King William the Lion granted the ferryboat of Montrose and its lands to Arbroath Abbey. These lands were probably what is now Ferryden farm, since Ferryden means 'the valley of the ferry'. This ferry operated for hundreds of years, ceasing when the first bridge across the river was completed in 1795. However, a new ferry service operated from at least the late nineteenth century to the middle of the twentieth century.

The village of Ferryden began to grow in the early 1700s when fishermen colonists from the north-east coast were encouraged to settle by Patrick Scott of Rossie. Local tradition suggests that as part of Scott's estate improvements he wished to encourage the growing white fish trade. Many fishermen are believed to have come from the Banff area, attracted by the deep anchorage and the abundance of mussel bait in the tidal basin. They brought names such as West and Coull with them, and coupled with local names such as Pert, Paton, Findlay and Mearns these are still much in evidence in the village today. The growth of the village really took off in the first three-quarters of the nineteenth century. There was a threefold growth in population during that period from 190 people to 679.

Until the middle of the eighteenth century most fishermen had operated from small boats that sailed close to the shore. The market for their catch was mainly local, sold in the Montrose fish market on the south side of what is now George Street. Further opportunities for the fleet arose as Dutch control over the North Sea waned throughout the eighteenth century. By 1785 the local minister, Revd James Paton, recorded that 38 Ferryden families operated six boats, with four men aboard each boat. Many of these fishermen found it necessary to supplement their incomes from other sources. A number of them would sail down to the Forth either with a cargo of fish or grain and return with a load of coal for local consumption. The smuggling of wine and other contraband was also a lucrative pastime. Many fishermen joined summer whaling expeditions which provided them with an income and freed them from the fear of the navy press-gang. Twenty-four fishermen from Ferryden and Usan served in the navy during the Napoleonic era, representing a grave drain on the village's manpower.

The Ferryden fishing fleet continued to grow throughout the eighteenth and much of the nineteenth century. Herring fishing was encouraged by the government, local landowners and merchants and the growth of this continued alongside line fishing for white fish such as haddock and ling. The establishment in 1825 of Joseph Johnston & Sons, salmon fishers, boosted trade as the company had wider interests such as the export of pickled cod, smoked haddock and herring to London and elsewhere. Johnston's also managed the source of bait, the mussel beds at Dun, while a Ferryden and Usan Fishermen's Association managed the beds at Rossie.

However, with such a dependence on one trade Ferryden's fortunes ebbed and flowed with those of fishing in general. Between the census of 1881 and that of 1901 the population increase showed a marked slowdown. By the early 1920s the Ferryden fleet was in serious decline. Like many other small fishing ports it had been unable to re-establish its market for herring after the end of World War I. Fishing from Ferryden had all but ceased by the 1930s, with only a handful of boats still operating.

After the Second World War Angus County Council planned to expand the village from 908 people to a population of 1,500. They saw its future as a dormitory for Montrose and for local agricultural workers. The county council built homes along the Inch Burn and shifted the focal point of the village towards the new playing fields. This trend continued into the 1970s and beyond.

Both Ferryden and Montrose's shipping trade was in the doldrums until the late 1960s when, in an effort to attract some of the new oil business to Montrose, the Inch Burn was filled in and the South Quay constructed. This has successfully attracted large shipping including the massive Star Line and oil support vessels to the area.

Ferryden is a picturesque village, clinging to the rocky south shore of the South Esk. Its houses are small and quaint, many with the old-fashioned forestairs which were once a very common architectural feature in Scotland but have long since vanished from the neighbouring burgh of Montrose. Over the years the village has been a favourite spot for painters and photographers. One of its unique features which intrigues artists and tourists alike is its washing lines stretching out over the sea. On a blowy day the clothes fill out and look like real people pegged out to dry. Tourists have been heard to speculate that locals might do this for their benefit, but it is simply a matter of practicality: few old Ferryden houses have gardens.

This charming view from 1936 shows the dwindling number of fishing boats in operation in the village at that date. One of the men in the foreground is Ferryboat Andrew; his ferry and its gangplank are at the water's edge to the right. Behind the ferry are two different types of fishing boat, a Fifie herring drifter and a smaller motor boat. To its left are three boats tied together; the small one in the middle is the *Betty*, owned by Mr Mearns. This vessel – and its owner – featured prominently in Edward Baird's painting of an almost identical scene in 1938. The concrete suspension-style bridge spans the entrance to the magnificent tidal basin, which is filled and emptied by the sea twice daily. During Ferryden's heyday, from the mid-nineteenth to the early twentieth centuries, its fisheries were extensive and provided employment for the entire village. In 1881 the population of 1,520 people supported 156 boats and 350 fishermen.

Rossie Island, or Inchbrayock as it was once known, was a quiet island with few houses until just after the First World War when it was developed by Montrose Town Council to relieve pressure on housing. The island was originally the site of an old Celtic church and a number of Pictish stones have been found there. During the early part of the twentieth century it housed a boatyard belonging to the Coaster Construction Company. The vessels in the picture may have been herring boats awaiting repairs. A mussel rake is just visible in the foreground and two of the boats are registered in Montrose, as denoted by the letters ME. The middle boat is an Arbroath (AH) vessel.

18585 MONTROSE FROM RAILWAY BRIDGE. *Poulton.*

It has been possible to cross the sluggish southern branch of the South Esk, called the Inch Burn, by bridge for over 200 years. In the 1790s Hercules Ross of Rossie, who owned the rights to the ferry, fought a long battle with Montrose Town Council for compensation for the loss of his ferry trade after the bridge opened in 1795. As a mark of protest, the ferrymen walked across the bridge carrying their oars draped in black to symbolise the death of the ferry. In addition to the bridge, a turnpike road was constructed leading up to it, and the result was that Ferryden was bypassed altogether. The Inchbridge tollhouse, with its semi-hexagonal west elevation, nestles at the lower right of the picture. It ceased to be a tollhouse during the 1830s but continues to be occupied as a house.

FUNERAL OF DR SCOTT CRAIG.

Despite its distance from Craig Parish Church, the churchyard surrounding the ruins of the medieval church of Inchbrayock on Rossie Island was the traditional burial place for Craig parish. A few headstones are visible at the upper right-hand corner of this picture. Before the building of the bridge it is believed that the dead were carried to the island at low tide when the burn was almost dry. Here Rossie Island appears rural and almost devoid of buildings. In 1893 Montrose Town Council bought the island from the Rossie estate for £27,000 and after 1919 began to develop it for housebuilding in a move to relieve pressure on the burgh's housing stock – and simultaneously to provide homes for workers at the Coaster Construction Company. Rossie Island has not been an island since the Inch Burn was filled in during the late 1970s, but the name lingers on. The bridge has now been replaced by a road and a roundabout.

FUNERAL OF DR SCOTT. CRAIG.

A large crowd of parishioners attended the funeral of Revd Dr Robert Scott of Craig Parish Church in May 1908. He took a great interest in the welfare of the young people in his parish and was well-loved by the community. Revd Dr Scott was chairman of both the school board of Craig and the Brechin local association of the Educational Institute of Scotland. He died in Edinburgh while attending the General Assembly and was brought back to his parish for burial in the churchyard on Rossie Island. The funeral party made its way down the hill from the parish church preceded by the village schoolchildren; the men of the parish followed the cortege. The photograph opposite shows the women lingering at the back of the procession. For many years in Scotland it was uncommon for women to attend funerals at all, a practice which still survives in some fishing villages. In the field in the background of this picture are old-fashioned style haystacks at Barns of Craig Farm.

UNVEILING OF CRAIG WAR MEMORIAL.

Craig war memorial was unveiled in October 1920 at a well-attended ceremony that was not affected by the poor weather. It was presided over by Captain Stansfeld of Dunninald and the Earl of Strathmore unveiled the memorial. Revd Bisset read the roll of the 60 men commemorated. They were drawn from all areas of the military: different regiments, the navy, naval reserve and colonial contingents. The small cottage on the left of this picture sat right on the shore and its site is now covered by the road into the village.

CRAIG WAR MEMORIAL, FERRYDEN, MONTROSE

87096 J.V.

The war memorial, a simple and elegant Celtic cross on a pedestal, originally stood at the site of the present rest garden at the end of Burnside Terrace, but was later moved to a new location at the King George V playing fields. This picture shows it on its original site, before the building of Burnside Terrace. The road on the right is now a footpath leading up to the houses surrounding Ferryden Primary School.

11

The Montrose lifeboat crew of 1895 photographed wearing cork life jackets (the Montrose lifeboat was traditionally crewed by a majority of men from Ferryden). This style of jacket had been in use since the 1850s, and many considered its bulk as a hindrance to movement. However, the insulating nature of cork – in addition to its buoyancy – saved many lives by retaining body heat and delaying hypothermia. In 1874 this helped to save four lifeboat crew who were washed overboard into icy cold water. The coxswain decided to first assist the brig *Henrietta* and then returned 25 minutes later to collect his crew. Cork life jackets remained in service until 1920.

The 1916 crew of the Montrose lifeboat seated outside the lifeboat shed displaying their service medals.

Daniel West was one of the many Ferryden men to serve on the lifeboat. He and his brother George, known by his bye-name of Menim, both served as coxswains. The coxswain was in sole charge of the lifeboat after its launch and it was his duty to decide on how to proceed with the rescue. Daniel received many certificates and medals for his service, some of which he is wearing here. He died in 1944.

The naming of a new lifeboat was an important occasion. On 18 September 1926 Elizabeth, Duchess of York (who had been born in Angus), named and launched the *John Russell*. It was a 45-foot Watson Cabin Class lifeboat and cost £8,273, the funds coming from a legacy left by Ann Russell of Manchester. Robert West was the first coxswain. The occasion was watched by thousands of people and the launch took place when the Duchess pulled a red, white and blue ribbon, breaking a bottle of Australian wine over the boat's bows. The festivities continued with a supper for the lifeboat crew in the Ferryden Fishermen's Hall. At the end of the day there was a spectacular display of fireworks which culminated in a portrait – in fireworks – of King George V and the Duke and Duchess of York.

The *John Russell* saw ten years service, rescuing 26 people in 32 launches.

On 12 July 1929 the local lifeboat crew were presented with vellum certificates to commemorate over 100 years of Ferryden's association with rescues at sea. A lifeboat station was established in Montrose in 1800, making it one of the first to be set up in the country. It was greatly needed as that same year 70 ships were lost between Easthaven and Redhead in one severe storm. The entrance to Montrose harbour was a difficult one in bad weather because of the presence of a barrier of hidden rocks and a great ridge of sand called the Annat Bank, so the need for a lifeboat was clear. From its earliest days, Ferryden fishermen offered their services, sometimes at great cost to themselves, and until the early part of the twentieth century the crew of the Montrose lifeboat was almost entirely made up of Ferrydeners. The Royal National Lifeboat Institution donated a boat to be kept on the south shore of the South Esk at Ferryden to enable the Ferryden crew-members to reach the station quickly. Although there is no longer such a boat at Ferryden, its boat shed can still be seen at the turning area at the end of River Street, and the village's connection with the lifeboat is still strong to this day.

LIFEBOATS, MONTROSE.

Despite the high number of Ferrydeners in the crew, the local lifeboats were stationed on the Montrose side of the South Esk, adjacent to the lower lighthouse. When the rocket was fired, signalling a ship was in danger, the crew had to row across the fast-flowing river to the lifeboat station (they kept their clothes and boots handy at night in case of emergency). The lifeboats had to be hauled to the water's edge and launched into the waves from a carriage, a process that took great skill and judgement on the part of the coxswain. If horses were required to pull the boat against the current towards a ship in distress on the Annat Bank, another rocket would go off signalling the need for them. Sometimes the horses were slow to arrive, and during one rescue in 1907 the crowd on the beach hauled the *Marianne Atherstone* (introduced in 1901) towards the Annat Bank themselves.

17

The Royal National Lifeboat Institution raised money to continue its work through a variety of fund-raising events such as Lifeboat Saturday, which became popular after 1900. This was a well-supported event, particularly because the money raised stayed in the area. It was used to pay the expenses of the coxswain and crew, to finance special awards and to alleviate the hardships of the families of men lost or injured on lifeboat service. Other methods of fund-raising included a special collection at the parish church, flag days and house-to-house collections. Ferryden and Montrose women have always taken a special interest in the lifeboat and are strong supporters of the Ladies Lifeboat Guild, formally founded in 1921. Their fund-raising events have become very varied over the years and have included a mannequin show of wedding dresses, sale of Christmas cards, Tupperware parties, jumble sales and other events, all of which have raised a great deal of money for the lifeboat service. The little girl in the centre of this picture is Georgina Paton.

In June 1953 the entire country celebrated the Coronation of Queen Elizabeth II. In Ferryden, a committee brought all the village groups together including the Masons, the Eastern Star, British Legion, Ferryden Free Church, the Brownies and the Bowling Club to coordinate their celebrations. Events organised included a best-kept garden competition, five-a-side football match, a church service, a treat of steak and kidney pie, trifle and ice cream for 120 old people, a Coronation Eve dance and a best-decorated house competition. Children were not forgotten, and the committee arranged for each child to receive a souvenir mug and attend a sports day at the playing fields, as well as participating in a fancy dress parade to the pier and enjoying a cinema show in the Fishermen's Hall. The children had to bring their own cups for the juice they were served. A temporary television aerial was erected on the roof of the senior school so that the villagers could watch what was the first live televised coronation of a British monarch.

This picture may show the Ferryden Sunday school picnic outing or a Templar parade. The Templars were a junior temperance organisation with Masonic features and provided activities for children such as magic lantern shows. They met in the old Fishermen's Hall on Beacon Terrace. This 1906 jaunt is seen passing Brownlow Place, led by two pipers from Rossie Reformatory. A Templar flag is flying. The gentleman to the right in the straw hat with the walking stick is the minister, Revd Fraser. The banner carried at the head of the procession is embroidered with the phrase 'With Charity For All'.

The company of Joseph Johnston & Sons was very important to both Montrose and Ferryden. Mr Johnston arrived in Montrose in 1825 as an agent for a Berwick salmon fisher, and soon established his own business sending salmon, smoked haddock and pickled cod to London, Glasgow and Russia. Herring became a major export in the 1880s and 1890s, and the company provided a market for much of the fish caught by the Ferryden fishing fleet, drawing up contracts with many of local fishermen to purchase their catches. (In 1857

a number of fishermen were caught breaking their contracts by secretly selling fish to other fish curers.) Local antiquarian J. G. Low related that crowds would gather to watch the Ferryden workers pack fish while singing hymns, and the quay between the company's premises and Pier Wynd was often covered with barrels 20 to 30 deep. Johnston's took an interest in the welfare of the Ferryden fisherfolk. In 1901 the company owned and rented out twelve properties in the village – in Beacon Terrace, King Street, Rossie Square, Southesk Place and William Street. In times of hardship, when the catch failed, Johnston's would organise fund-raising concerts to help the families of fishermen. This photograph shows the fish cadgers' outing to Edzell Castle. They brought their wives and children with them and invited Mr James Johnston to accompany them.

Originally mussels were gathered and shelled by families for their own use, but as time went by the mussel beds began to be managed commercially, and fishermen could have mussels delivered to them, thereby avoiding the time-consuming job of gathering them. A further development of this was commercial mussel shelling, which was maintained by Johnston's. This picture dates from the 1970s and probably shows a Johnston's employee.

Some fishing boats were built and maintained in the village, although many were constructed in Montrose by Joseph Johnston. Boats were also built on Rossie Island. In 1901 the Ferryden Fishermen's Association owned a workshop on Usan Road where boats were repaired. Ferryden's population included carpenters, sailmakers and net makers and menders, so the fishing community could be largely self-sufficient. The cost of a new boat was substantial. In 1904 the trawler *Seagull* (ME 24) sank after a collision with another fishing boat. She was insured for £490 but had cost between £600 and £700 to build. In the event the insurance didn't even cover the cost of her gear.

It was the custom in fishing villages to have a naming ceremony for newly-built boats. A large party would assemble to see the boat launched and celebrations would take place in the local tavern afterwards. The master boat-builder sometimes inserted a coin into the planking to bring prosperity to the boat, and at the vessel's christening the local minister would bless the boat to bring her success in her work and to ask for the safety of her crew. Boats' names often followed a trend and might be chosen from themes such as flowers, names of members of the family or astronomical names. This boat-naming ceremony took place at Usan.

A fisherman tars his boat, assisted by a young boy. If a boat was leaky it would be laid up on the banks of the Inch Burn and the mud allowed to get into all the gaps between the planks. When this dried out it provided a good base for the tar. The foreshore in front of Brownlow Place, to the left of the shed in the middle, was the pick-up point for the ferry. Two paths provided access to the beach. On the left-hand side there were steps while the other path was a smooth slope down which nets could be taken to the shore in a bogey. The foreshore was a favourite place for children to play, with the low walls at the bottom of the sheds a favourite spot. The row of houses on the right have been replaced by Southesk Court, a sheltered housing complex.

Here many Ferryden fishing boats can be seen moored on both banks of the sluggish Inch Burn. The Ferryden fleet caught a variety of fish including cod, ling, haddock, skate, flounders and turbot. Lobsters and salmon were also caught in the South Esk. In the late 1790s, a boat's crew would receive three farthings for every pound of white fish caught. Ferryden fishermen used a number of different fishing methods including line fishing from skiffs, great line fishing from larger sail boats, seine net fishing and trawling. On the right-hand side of the photograph are the former green fields of Rossie Island which were developed for housing from the 1920s onwards.

In the late nineteenth century some local fishermen made the transition to steam drifters, which could carry larger nets and reach more distant fishing grounds than sailing vessels. By 1885 at least two steam drifters were owned and operated by Joseph Johnston, although when the company tried to reduce the wages of the fishermen that worked on them they went on strike. There were only three steam drifters registered at the port of Montrose in 1890, the first of which was the SS *Swift* (pictured here). In three trips to sea, in one week, the three vessels landed 294 hundredweight of haddock and plaice plus 130 large cod. These larger boats generally fished between ten and thirty miles out to sea while the smaller vessels worked at three to nine miles. They experienced competition from the numerous steam trawlers from other ports and regularly complained – through the Fisheries Office in Montrose – about steam trawlers from Dundee working only one or two miles off the coast within protected waters.

John Brown, a photographer based at 14 High Street, Montrose, travelled with the herring fleet to take photographs of the men at work. He was on good terms with many of the fishermen, sending them postcards of his own work to ask them how their girlfriends were. This photograph of the SS *Swift* (ME 167), taken around 1907, shows a relaxed crew shooting the nets.

HERRING FISHING, SOME HERRING

Another photograph by John Brown of Montrose showing a vessel, probably also the SS *Swift*, hauling in its catch of herring. The weather conditions are harsher than in the previous picture and the crew are wearing sou'westers. Postcards such as this one were sent in large numbers by fishermen when away for the herring fishing as a quick and easy way of keeping in touch with families at home.

Margaret West posed for this photograph in her traditional blue and white striped skirt, holding a net and standing next to a Ferryden-made basket. Her blouse is elaborately embroidered, and she wears a lace knit scarf around her head and shoulders. Fisher girls did not wear coats. The traditional job of the fishwife was to assist her husband by baiting the lines with mussels. Originally these had to be gathered from the Basin all year round and then shelled before the 1,200 hooks could be baited with two mussels each. This duty was done in addition to looking after the home and children. Life for women became a little easier in the twentieth century when mussels started to be delivered to a fisherman's own mussel bed, a round stone structure on the foreshore (although this service had to be paid for). Margaret may have posed for her portrait in Hartlepool, Scarborough or Great Yarmouth as young, unmarried fisher girls followed the herring fleet where they earned money packing the herring in barrels. They worked in crews of three, two gutters and one packer. The wages were good and the girls often used them to purchase goods such as witch balls, ornaments and china for their wedding chests.

Local fisher girls followed the Ferryden herring fleet up and down the east coast as it pursued the migratory fish. This group of girls posed for a formal portrait to take home as a souvenir of their time away from home – they may well also have used copies of the photograph as postcards to write home and let the family know the success, or otherwise, of the Ferryden fleet's season. The girls would work in teams of three to gut, salt and pack the freshly caught herring in barrels. It was hard work but made easier by the camaraderie of the team. An older aunt or unmarried woman would often make up part of the team to act as chaperone.

The Ferryden fishing girls who followed the herring fleet to pack the fish in Great Yarmouth or Scarborough for the July to September season had to work hard. Here they are seen 'heading up the barrels'. Herring had to be salted within twenty-four hours of being caught to obtain the coveted Scottish Crown brand mark. Every day, for up to eleven days, layers of fish and salt were added to the barrel before it was finally sealed with a wooden lid and the brand mark applied. Much of the catch was exported to the Baltic states and Germany, but demand died with the outbreak of World War I.

This picture shows a typical Ferryden fishing family. In fishing communities people often lived with their extended families, and the 1891 census for Ferryden shows many households comprising grandparents, aunts, married sons and unmarried daughters all under the same roof. It is said that Miss Ross of Rossie once took a stroll through the village and was appalled at the size of the families the fisher women had to manage. Around 1834, she endowed an Infant School to teach children from three years of age until they were old enough to attend the Den School. Places were always filled and many mothers tried to sneak in underage children. This was the first nursery school in Scotland. The school's most memorable teacher was Jessie Coull, headmistress for over 25 years. She was known as the spiritual mother of the village and on the day of her funeral in 1912 the fishing boats set sail with their flags at half mast.

Where King Street turns into River Street, at the junction with Victoria Square, there is a slipway down to the beach where small boats were once beached amongst the shelter of the rocks. The sheds which lined the riverside here were used for a number of purposes including as wash houses, for fish curing, and as stores for equipment and boilers. In this picture Ferrydeners are shown working with creels, lobster pots, baskets and fish crates. The buildings immediately to the left still exist today but those on River Street have disappeared, and benches now occupy this spot. As few houses in Ferryden had gardens these open-air work areas were of great importance to the community, also providing an outdoor meeting place for neighbours. One of the village's public wells was situated in the area to the left. For many years guaranteeing an adequate and safe water supply was a problem for the village. In 1886 a typhoid epidemic caused many deaths during the herring season. Revd Mitchell queried the colour of the water and had it sent to Edinburgh for analysis, as a result of which the outbreak was traced to a defective water pipe bringing the supply from Rossie Braes. During the epidemic barrels of clean water were transported from Montrose, while the sick were treated in the Fishermen's Hall which was temporarily converted into a fever hospital.

The foreshore in front of Brownlow Place was the terminal for the ferry. The tarred huts to the left are the last remaining ones in the village – the one in the centre of the picture was formerly used as the beer cellar for the Esk Hotel. It is long gone and the foreshore garden now occupies its site. Today the gap between the two sets of huts houses another wooden building, Ferryden post office and shop, the last remaining shop in the village. The row of houses is home to two pubs, the Esk Hotel and the Ferrydener, built in 1973.

FERRYDEN, MONTROSE 87097

A busy scene at Brownlow Place. The ladies in the foreground are baiting lines. During the nineteenth century Ferryden was known for its heavy-drinking fishermen. Revd Brewster helped to change that by inspiring a fervent temperance movement, although other people argue that the presence of the village police station from 1859 did more to eradicate the drinking culture of the villagers. Stricter controls over licensing arrangements may also have helped, and by May 1885 there was only one licensed house in the village.

In the nineteenth century the ferryboat was reintroduced under the auspices of the Ferryden Ferryboat Company Limited. It operated from the foreshore, where the garden is situated today, and was well-used by Ferryden girls who found work in Paton's Mill in Montrose. They worked in the mill until they married a fishermen, after which they were likely to be occupied outdoors baiting the lines. Initially the ferryboat company used old style cobles before introducing a motor boat. In the summer the 'official' ferry had competition from casual ferryboats that snatched its passengers. One ferryman, Arthur Craig, lobbied for the withdrawal of the Sunday service, while on another occasion his religious fervour led him to give one boy a free passage from Montrose when he saw he had purchased a psalm book. More often, however, the ferrymen encountered problems such as those experienced by modern-day school bus drivers. Their tempers were tried by spirited young passengers who had to be threatened – midstream – to behave well!

As the twentieth century dawned many Ferryden girls began to abandon the hard life of the fisher lassie. Fishing was in decline and new forms of employment had to be sought. The 1891 census shows a large number of fishermen's daughters turning to millwork, while the outbreak of war in 1914 offered many girls the chance to work in areas which had previously been denied them. A large number were employed in the many Montrose factories which were easily accessible by ferry. Most of the ferry passengers were women and many returned to Ferryden for their lunch break.

MONTROSE FROM FERRYDEN

B 7846

A pier or landing stage has existed at this location since the early thirteenth century, some years after Arbroath Abbey was granted the right to operate a ferry service across the South Esk on this important north-south route. By the 1800s the original pier had become inadequate for local boats. It was enlarged around 1832 by the laird, Hercules Ross of Rossie, but was still too small for most vessels. In later centuries crossing on a Sunday was banned by the Montrose Kirk Session although this was a very popular day for travelling in the late nineteenth century. The pier illustrated here remained in use until the South Quay was constructed in the early 1970s. It is now home to large vessels such as the *Big Orange XVIII*.

A group of Ferrydeners stands outside one of the village's distinctive houses. The man leaning on the cart was Mr West, known as Wastie, whose shop was located behind the photographer. On Wastie's right is Simon Paton, the signalman at Usan, while Mrs West and Willy Mitchell, the rag and bone man from Montrose who had only one good leg, stand to his left. Willy travelled around with his horse and cart exchanging balloons and cheap ornaments for rags and jam jars. This photograph may have been taken in William Street.

The inhabitants of William Street turned out in force to be included in this picture of their street. The backs of these houses face on to the river. The shed at the end of the street has gone but the house with the outside stair still retains this feature.

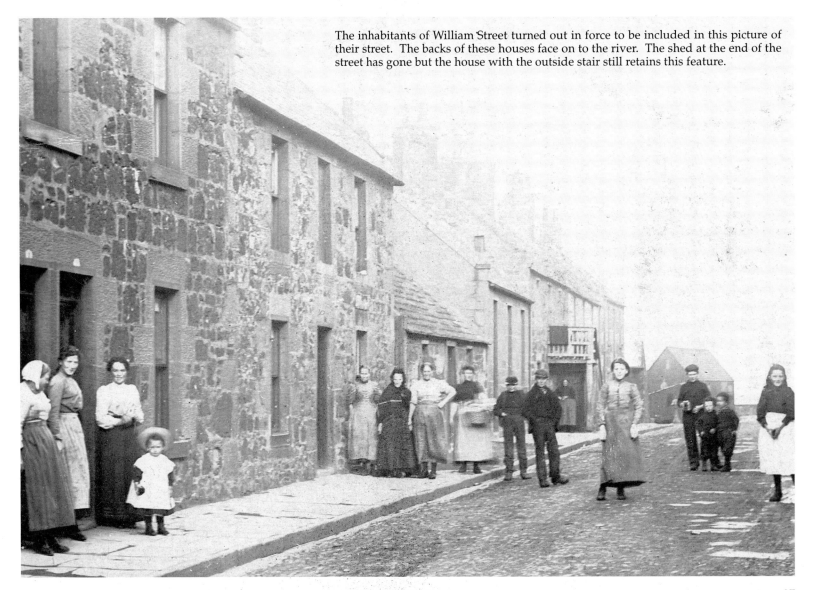

Ferryden had a number of schools, the largest of which, on Usan Road, was commonly known as the Den School. In 1909 the entire school lined up in the playground to have their photograph taken. John Speirs Burt, a strict but benevolent man, was headmaster between 1912 and 1951. He married fellow Den School teacher Miss Peddie. The Den School was the senior school and was in use until 1974 when the modern primary school was opened.

Over the years the post office has been located in a number of properties in the village. Its first location was at the foot of Usan Road and by the early twentieth century it was to be found on part of the ground floor of this house in Rossie Square. Mr Williams, who ran it, sold a wide a variety of other goods too. Later Tom Findlay ran the post office from William Street, and today it is located opposite the Esk Hotel. Ferryden shopkeepers were kindly people. According to local folklore children often forget what their mothers had sent them out to get. If they cried, Tom Findlay at the William Street post office would soothe them with half a stick of rock and send them home with a variety of supplies, reassuring them that everything would be fine.

A.1975   BURNSIDE, FERRYDEN.

Before the Inch Burn was filled in to form the South Quay the residents of Burnside Terrace had fabulous views over the river to Rossie Island and the Basin beyond. It is said that the houses on Burnside Terrace have very deep cellars, a feature connected either with the fact that they were constructed during wartime or the result of structural necessity.

A view of a tranquil Inch Burn dividing Rossie Island from Ferryden. Many of the low cottages on the right at the foot of the church have now been built up to two storeys. The area around the pier is in the middle of the picture, and the view stretches to the end of William Street on the left.

This picture was taken from the Montrose side of the South Esk and shows the Mission Hall, now the parish church hall, in the centre. A number of local groups meet here, including the new generation of Ferrydeners who gather at the playgroup. The fields above the village have now been built on to create housing at Hill View, while the houses on the right have been obscured by Annat House, part of the harbour's South Quay complex.

An atmospheric photograph by John Fraser (see also the front cover), showing a dredger at work in the South Esk. The river is dredged every year around May. In 1975 the vessel doing the dredging developed a hole in its suction pipe, causing stones to bombard the houses in River Street and resulting in some damage.

The core of Craig House is a twelfth century castle. The Rossie estate was quite extensive during the eighteenth century when it was owned by the powerful Scott family who encouraged the first settlers from the north to Ferryden. In 1784 it was purchased for £35,000 by Hercules Ross. He had made a fortune in Jamaica and used his money to fulfil the eighteenth century dream of retiring back to Scotland and purchasing a respectable estate and position in life. Ross and his family were great benefactors within the parish, and his wife funded a new church at a cost of £2,000 which she gifted to the parish in 1799. Ross built a large, modern mansion for himself called Rossie Castle further up Rossie Braes and the family moved out of Craig House in 1800. Eventually Craig House was sold off separately from the remainder of the estate, and while Rossie Castle was demolished in 1949 Craig House is still inhabited.

In 1869 Colonel MacDonald of Rossie estate donated an area of land around the west end of the Basin – just beyond the Inch Bridge – for use as a public park. Rossie Gardens, MacDonald's Park, or the Widie as it was variously known was a favourite destination for a Sunday afternoon walk. The gardens were landscaped with a winding path and bridges over the streams. Seats were provided and areas were laid out with shrubs. There were swings for the children and even a maypole, and an area was cleared as a football pitch. When the Rossie estate was sold the park fell into disuse and by 1921 was becoming overgrown, although despite this many Ferryden youngsters still enjoyed it as a place to play football. Little trace of the park is visible today.

Ferryden farm is situated at the top of the Den, on Usan Road. It may have been part of the lands granted to Arbroath Abbey along with the rights to the ferry in the twelfth century. This line-up of farm workers and their families is believed to have been taken at the farm in the late nineteenth century.

CRAIG TERRACE, FERRYDEN.

In the 1930s Angus County Council decided that the future of Ferryden lay in it serving as a dormitory for workers in Montrose and local agricultural workers. They built new housing to the west of the existing village, including Craig Terrace, and this westward expansion has continued to the present day. This led to some unexpected results. In 1944 James Davidson, Fishery Officer, petitioned the War Department for permission to purchase an alarm clock for a Ferryden fisherman who could not get his crew mates to wake him up in the morning. They said it was too far for them to walk!

SCURDYNESS, MONTROSE.

The rocks around the coast in Craig parish are volcanic, emanating from an extinct underwater volcano many miles out to sea. Despite being hard and tough to split, Scurdy rock has long been quarried. Rare blue agates are found in this area and on Sunday mornings agate hunters are a common sight on the shore. One quarried area came to be known as Johnnie Main's harbour after a well-known eighteenth century smuggler of gin and other contraband. Johnnie often used women as carriers. It is said that when an excise man approached one of the women she pretended she was in labour, and while he returned to the village to get help she gave birth to her cargo of alcohol in Johnnie Main's harbour! John Low's quarry, on the far side of the lighthouse, provided a natural swimming pool where many local children learned to swim.